Original title:
Oaken Scuffs Across the Phoenix Yard

Copyright © 2025 Swan Charm
All rights reserved.

Author: Sebastian Sarapuu
ISBN HARDBACK: 978-1-80563-465-2
ISBN PAPERBACK: 978-1-80564-986-1

Charcoal Silhouettes Against the Light

In the twilight's gentle grace,
Shadows dance, a fleeting trace.
Whispers soft as secrets shared,
Moments lost, yet deeply cared.

Branches stretch with stories old,
Beneath the sky, a canvas bold.
Glimmers shine through leaves so fine,
Crafting tales, a grand design.

Winds of change begin to play,
Carrying ghosts of yesterday.
Laughter echoes through the air,
Promises made, a tender prayer.

Echoes meet the fading glow,
Where stars awaken, soft and slow.
Each heartbeat, a note in time,
Painting dreams, both grand and sublime.

As darkness wraps the world in peace,
Charcoal figures find release.
In the light, our shadows dwell,
A silent spell, a mystic well.

When Nature Finds Its Voice Again

Amidst the whispers of the trees,
Soft melodies drift on the breeze.
The flowers bloom in vibrant hues,
A symphony of nature ensues.

The streams, they giggle, dance, and play,
The sun awakens a brand new day.
In every corner, life ignites,
As hope returns to earth's delights.

Chronicles of Flame and Renewal

In shadows deep where embers lay,
A tale of fire meets the day.
From ashes rise the whispers bold,
A story of the brave retold.

With every crackle, every spark,
New dreams emerge from lands once dark.
The cycle spins, both fierce and kind,
In flames, a truth we seek to find.

A Journey Through the Singed Woods

Through woods charred black, where silence weeps,
A path of strength through sorrow creeps.
Old branches twist in darkened grace,
Yet life returns, a warm embrace.

The phoenix flutters in the glade,
In every shadow, hope is laid.
As time unfurls its gentle hand,
Renewal blooms across the land.

The Beauty of Scars on Earth

With every scar, a tale of woe,
Yet beauty shines in what we know.
The earth adorned in rugged lace,
Each mark, a step in time and space.

From sorrow's depth, new life will rise,
In aching beauty, truth resides.
Embrace the flaws, for they are real,
In scars, the heart begins to heal.

Footprints in the Charcoal Dust

In the silence, shadows creep,
Footprints left in whispers deep.
Charcoal dust upon the ground,
Stories lost, yet still are found.

Echoes of a fire's past,
In the twilight, memories cast.
Each step sings of what once was,
In the glow, the mind still buzzes.

A Symphony of Rebirth

Beneath the ashes, life will bloom,
A symphony dispels the gloom.
Notes of hope in every heart,
From the shadows, dreams depart.

Softly sung, the earth awakes,
Melodies of love it makes.
New beginnings, bright and clear,
In every sound, the world draws near.

Twilight Against the Burnt Bark

Against the bark, the twilight sighs,
A gentle kiss from darkening skies.
Soft hues of purple blend with gray,
As day bids night to come and play.

Cracks and crevices, stories told,
By nature's ink, in colors bold.
The air is thick, with dreams set free,
In whispered breaths, their legacy.

The Dance of Ashes and Roots

Ashes swirl, a spectral dance,
In the moonlight, take a chance.
Roots entwined, they rise and sway,
Secrets of the earth at play.

In every flicker, shadows tease,
Echoes carried on the breeze.
Nature's pulse beneath the ground,
In this waltz, true peace is found.

Where Flames Once Roamed Freely

Where flames once danced in wild delight,
The ashes whisper tales of night.
A world reborn, yet still it sighs,
Beneath the grey and shifting skies.

The scars of fire hold secrets old,
In embered hearts, the embers bold.
Yet life persists, though shadows loom,
A fragile hope in twilight's gloom.

With every breeze, the stories flow,
Of battles lost, of seeds to sow.
From charred remains, new dreams arise,
In hues of fire beneath the skies.

Regrowth Amongst the Ruins

Amongst the stones where legends lay,
New green shoots reach for the day.
Through crumbled walls, life finds a way,
With sunlight guiding, brightening the gray.

In quiet corners, hope is sewn,
Amongst the shards, new seeds are grown.
A tapestry of past and now,
The earth remembers, and still avows.

Each grassy blade, a tale retold,
Of dreams once lost, now brave and bold.
In every nook, a songbird trills,
A symphony of nature's wills.

Tender Shoots from the Blackened Soil

From blackened soil, where shadows creep,
Tender shoots rise, their promise deep.
With sunlit kisses, they unfold,
In colors bright, against the cold.

Each tiny leaf, a sign of cheer,
A dance of life that draws us near.
In quiet strength, they stretch towards light,
Defying darkness, taking flight.

With every raindrop's gentle kiss,
They whisper dreams of what is bliss.
In circles vast, the earth complies,
As life awakens, and sorrow dies.

Rustling Leaves of the Reclaimed

Rustling leaves in whispers sway,
Of battles fought, of shadows gray.
In colors bright, they catch the sun,
A symphony of life begun.

Amongst the roots, old stories weave,
In every breeze, the past believed.
With every rustle, tales revive,
In the heart of all, they come alive.

The forest breathes, a hopeful song,
Where once was grief, now life belongs.
In every branch, the hope is clear,
A love of earth that draws us near.

Nature's Palette Post-Incendiarism

Vivid hues emerge from ash,
Colors dance where shadows clash.
Amongst the cinders, life will sprout,
Nature's brush paints all about.

Healing whispers through the trees,
Softly swaying in the breeze.
From charred remains, new stories bloom,
In every corner, life finds room.

Golden rays pierce through the smoke,
As silence hums, the forest spoke.
Past scars will fade, new dreams ascend,
Nature's cycle shall not end.

Here, the earth finds strength to mend,
In sunlight's warmth, all wounds extend.
In vibrant strokes, it paints anew,
With patience, life will always cue.

From fire's blaze the seeds ignite,
In darkened nights, we seek their light.
Together, they shall rise and weave,
A tapestry the heart believes.

Growth Amongst Flickering Flames

In ember's glow, a dance takes flight,
Life struggles hard to seek the light.
Fingers grab at fleeting dreams,
While hope shimmers in fragile beams.

From ashes rise, new shoots emerge,
Defying odds, they surge and surge.
Courage blooms on barren ground,
In whispered breaths, their strength is found.

Leaves unfurl towards the sun,
Each moment lived, a battle won.
With flickering flames, they intertwine,
The spirit's spark, forever shines.

In vibrant hues, the past shall fade,
While courage sows a grand parade.
Amongst the chaos, beauty breathes,
A tapestry that softly weaves.

As chaos hums, the world resets,
Amongst the flames, no regrets.
Together in the fire's embrace,
Life finds its way, renewed with grace.

Breathing Life into Blackened Places

In blackened realms where shadows creep,
Life stirs below, begun to leap.
Roots stretch deep, caressed by night,
With each small movement, dreams take flight.

From charred remains, the whispers call,
A symphony of rise and fall.
With every sigh, the earth revives,
In bitter soil, resilience thrives.

Beneath the grim and dusty haze,
A spark ignites forgotten days.
In every crack, the green begins,
Where silence dwelt, new life now spins.

With tender hands, the earth we nurture,
In every heart, there's a new future.
Amongst the fallen, strength restored,
In blackened places, hope is poured.

Together we weave a tranquil dream,
From ash and soot, a vibrant gleam.
As life unfolds with tender grace,
Breathing love into every space.

The Gentle Tug of Renewal

A beckoning force beneath the ground,
Pulling life up from where it's found.
Each budding leaf, a gentle sigh,
As nature whispers, 'Time to rise.'

The earth exhales in softest tones,
In secret groves, the spirit roans.
Roots entwine in loving embrace,
In every heartbeat, a sacred place.

Hope's gentle tug in every stream,
Filling the world with wondrous dreams.
While flickers of life dart through the air,
Renewal waits, a love affair.

With every dawn, a vibrant scene,
In colors bold, the life unseen.
From whispered winds to golden rays,
Each moment speaks of brighter days.

So here we stand amidst the bloom,
In every heart, there's space to room.
As gentle tugs guide us on our way,
Life begins anew, come what may.

Chains of Flames and Roots Intertwined

In shadows deep where embers glow,
The roots entwine, a tale of woe.
Chains of flames, they flicker bright,
In silent whispers, they seek the light.

The forest sighs, its secrets kept,
With every spark, a promise wept.
Through tangled vines and fiery breath,
Life intertwines, defying death.

A dance of ash and green anew,
The bonds of earth and flame ring true.
In summer's heat, through winter's chill,
Resilient hearts ignite the will.

Twisted branches reach so high,
Holding dreams against the sky.
In every spark, a story lives,
Of hope renewed, the heart forgives.

So let the flames rise, fierce and bold,
For in their warmth, the world is gold.
Chains of flames and roots that bind,
A legacy of fate entwined.

Tales Embedded in the Grain of Strength

In whispers soft, the wood does speak,
Of strength, of courage, of hearts unique.
Tales embedded in its grain,
Of love's sweet joy and bitter pain.

With every knot, a secret held,
A memory where laughter swelled.
Through storms that raged, it stood so tall,
In silent pride, it faced them all.

The ax does strike, the ripples spread,
Yet life persists where once it bled.
For from the earth, the roots extend,
A timeless tale that will not end.

With every ring, a year revealed,
In ancient bark, the truth concealed.
From tiny seeds, great oaks arise,
A testament beneath the skies.

So gather 'round, hear nature's song,
In every grain, where we belong.
In strength anew, our hearts are tuned,
To tales of life, forever crooned.

Wildflowers in the Wake of a Blaze

In charred remains where silence lingers,
Wildflowers rise on gentle fingers.
A tapestry of colors bright,
Emerging boldly from the night.

From ashes dark, the beauty grows,
In nature's grace, the spirit flows.
Where flames once danced, and shadows played,
New life awakens, unafraid.

Each petal speaks of battles fought,
Lessons learned and wisdom sought.
Through golden sun or drenching rain,
Their roots push deep, despite the pain.

With fragrant whispers on the breeze,
They sway and twist among the trees.
In every bloom, a story's spun,
Of hope reborn when day is done.

So let the fires rage if they must,
For in their wake, we learn to trust.
Wildflowers rise, a vibrant call,
From embered ground, they conquer all.

Songs of Regrowth in the Elemental Dance

In twilight's glow, the elements play,
With earth and fire in grand ballet.
Songs of regrowth swirl like mist,
In nature's palms, we gladly twist.

The wind shall carry, the rain shall nurture,
In every storm, we find adventure.
With roots that dive and branches spread,
Through trials tough, our paths are tread.

A melody of life resounds,
In every heartbeat, love abounds.
The soil holds secrets, deep and vast,
In every moment, echoes last.

The flame ignites, the water weeps,
In union strong, the spirit leaps.
The dance of change, so wild and free,
In cycles spun, we cease to flee.

So let us sing, in harmony,
In every breath, our tapestry.
Songs of regrowth, a timeless trance,
Within the light of this dance.

Rustic Echoes in a Fire's Embrace

In the hearth where shadows play,
Whispers dance in soft array.
Timber crackles, stories sigh,
In this warmth, dreams never die.

Embers glow, a gentle light,
Guiding hearts through darkest night.
Flickering tales of old and new,
In the fire's veil, spirits brew.

Hushed reflections, moments caught,
In this solace, peace is sought.
Rustic echoes of laughter blend,
Memories cherished, never end.

Outside, the world may rush and race,
Yet here we find a sacred space.
In the flames, we are reborn,
Embraced by warmth, forever worn.

So gather round, let stories soar,
In the grip of fire's core.
Rustic echoes, sweet and low,
Keep us grounded, help us grow.

The Resilience of Nature's Call

Beneath the soil, whispers grow,
Roots entwined, a timeless flow.
Each new sprout, a tale untold,
In nature's grip, life unfolds.

Storms may howl, and winds may wail,
Yet through the dark, the brave prevail.
A flower blooms in battle's wake,
Resilience sings, no hearts will break.

Stone and vine, each bond is strong,
In this wild, we all belong.
Seasons shift, the dance goes on,
Life's great symphony plays on.

Leaves may fall, but forests rise,
Underneath the vast, bright skies.
Nature's call, a sacred plea,
In every heartbeat, wild and free.

So let us tread, both bold and small,
Answering the earth's sweet call.
For in our hearts, we find the way,
Resilience grows with each new day.

When Ash Meets Oak in Twilight's Embrace

When twilight falls, the shadows creep,
The earth takes breath, the world in sleep.
Ashen skies paint scenes in grey,
While oaks stand firm, come what may.

In the hush, a soft refrain,
Whispers travel through the lane.
Branches entwined, a gentle hold,
Echoes warm, their tales unfold.

Stars awaken, dimly lit,
Each twinkle where the branches sit.
In this dance of night and day,
As time drifts softly, far away.

Rustling leaves, a tender sound,
Secrets whispered all around.
When ash meets oak, old friends unite,
In twilight's cradle, soft and bright.

So pause awhile, let night extend,
In nature's arms, we find a friend.
As shadows merge and silence sways,
We'll linger longer, through the haze.

Forest Secrets Under Celestial Watch

In moonlit glades where fairies play,
A symphony of night holds sway.
Beneath the boughs, a hush prevails,
In whispers soft, the forest tales.

Stars alight in velvet skies,
Glimmers dance in wild disguise.
Each secret housed in petals bright,
Beneath the cloak of deepest night.

Footsteps light on mossy ground,
Nature's pulse a gentle sound.
Old trees cradle stories true,
Guardians of what once we knew.

Silver beams through branches weave,
Shadows whisper, nights deceive.
In the wild, where darkness dwells,
Lies the wisdom in the spells.

So breathe it in, this sacred place,
Under the stars, let worries grace.
In forest depths, our dreams take flight,
Secrets held in the soft twilight.

Tales Woven in Earth and Ember

In the forest where whispers weave,
Dreams and stories softly breathe,
Roots entangle time's embrace,
A tapestry of magic in this place.

Brimming brooks sing of old lore,
Carried beneath the tree's core,
Echoes of voices lost in song,
In shadows where the heart feels strong.

Embers dance with gentle light,
Flickering hopes that take their flight,
Each spark a wish cast to the stars,
A bond unbroken despite the scars.

The moon watches with a silver gaze,
Guiding paths through woven maze,
Every step a tale unwinds,
In the quiet, the heart finds.

From soot and soil, magic blooms,
In hidden nooks where darkness looms,
A story forged through fire and rain,
Where love and loss truly remain.

Beyond the Flames, a New Dawn

Beyond the flames, a whisper calls,
A dawning light that softly falls,
Amidst the ashes, life shall seem,
A fragile thread, a glimmering dream.

The morning breaks, revealing skies,
Where hope beneath the sorrow lies,
Each shadow flees the sun's embrace,
In golden glow, we find our place.

Winds carry stories untold,
Of battles fought and hearts so bold,
With every gust, the past shall sigh,
As new souls rise and old ones fly.

Dewdrops cradle yesterday's tears,
While laughter echoes, calming fears,
A journey starts with each new dawn,
As light unfolds, despair is gone.

In this rebirth, we find our song,
Melodies where we all belong,
Beyond the flames, our hearts align,
In unity, a brighter sign.

Resurgence in Shadows

In the dark, where secrets lie,
Whispers bloom, and memories sigh,
Amidst the shadows, hearts ignite,
A flicker of hope, a spark of light.

Veils of night, they softly fold,
Embracing stories yet to be told,
Each passing hour, a chance reborn,
In twilight's grasp, we feel the morn.

The dance of dreams in muted hue,
Revealing truths we thought we knew,
With each heartbeat, strength we find,
A thread of courage intertwined.

Through tangled paths, the echoes roam,
In every sigh, a way back home,
The sun will rise, and shadows wane,
In resurgence, we break the chain.

From whispered fears, new wings shall sprout,
In the silent night, we hear the shout,
Together we rise, unchained and vast,
In shadows, our strength is steadfast.

Life's Tender Resilience Amidst Ruin

Amidst the ruins, life will bloom,
In silent corners, dispelling gloom,
Tender shoots where hope is sown,
In scars of earth, resilience grown.

From shattered dreams, a new pulse calls,
With whispers soft as gentle falls,
Each fragile heartbeat sings its song,
In broken places, we belong.

Beneath the weight of every stone,
A spirit soars, resilient, grown,
Finding light in darkest days,
In life's embrace, we learn to gaze.

Through trials faced, we rise again,
In every piece, a tale of pain,
Yet woven strong with threads of grace,
In ruins, we find our rightful place.

So gather close, where hope ignites,
In every heart, a spark of flights,
Amidst the ruin, life will stand,
In tender strength, we walk hand in hand.

Hushed Whispers in the Charred Silence

In the ashes, secrets lie,
Birds sing soft, though shadows sigh.
Echoes dance on thinning air,
Whispers linger, everywhere.

Flickers of light pierce the gloom,
Silent tales and thoughts entomb.
Holding breaths where silence reigns,
In the stillness, hope remains.

Footsteps tread on embered ground,
Lost in dreams, the past resound.
Hushed the cries of days gone by,
In charcoal haze, a muted sky.

Brittle1 leaves collect the dew,
Cloaked in shadows, life renews.
Courage finds its way back home,
In the quiet, spirits roam.

Awake anew, the world shall see,
In the burnt, the heart set free.
Hushed whispers in silent nights,
Ignite the flame through faded sights.

Soft Petals on a Smoldering Canvas

Gentle blooms in twilight's grasp,
Upon the ashes, beauty clasp.
Petals drift on breezes sweet,
In decay, resurgence greet.

Colors blend in dusky hues,
Nature weaves her vibrant muse.
From the fire's fierce embrace,
Emerges life with quiet grace.

Canvas of char and fleeting light,
A symphony of day and night.
Fragile blooms break through the sore,
Painting hope forevermore.

Amidst the wreckage, life will thread,
Soft shades rise where shadows spread.
With every petal, stories flow,
From the embers, life will grow.

In the tapestry that fate designs,
New worlds bloom where darkness shines.
Soft petals on the canvas lay,
Whispering dreams of brighter days.

Tendrils of Green from Charred Remnants

From the blackened earth they rise,
Tendrils stretch to greet the skies.
Through the cracks, new life will peek,
In the ruins, nature speaks.

Green whispers twine through jagged stone,
Vowing not to stand alone.
Where the fire claimed its toll,
Beats the heart of green and goal.

Leaves unfurl in tender grace,
Finding strength in empty space.
Against the night, they strive anew,
Colors beam where shadows grew.

Every fiber, once laid bare,
Sings of life—a fervent flare.
Charred remains will not despise,
For resilience dares to rise.

In the midst of all that's lost,
Nature's melody is embossed.
Tendrils of green in brave ballet,
Chart a course for a new day.

The Heartbeat of Resilience

In a world once gripped by pain,
Hope beats on, a steady rain.
Through the storms and fiery trials,
Life endures with endless smiles.

With each pulse, the dream will wake,
In the shadows, light will break.
Through every tear and whispered word,
The heartbeat of strength is heard.

Mountains may crumble, rivers bend,
But spirits rise; they'll never end.
In the heart, deep waters swell,
Resilience casts its faithful spell.

From each stumble, lessons bloom,
In the darkness, courage loom.
Every heartbeat, every breath,
Dances free, defying death.

So let the world know of this fight,
In each struggle, shines a light.
The journey weaves a timeless thread,
The heartbeat of all that is fed.

The Croon of Healing Haven

In shadows cast by willow's weep,
The gentle croon starts soft and deep.
A melody of solace sings,
In hearts where tender healing springs.

With every note, the spirits soar,
Through fields where whispered dreams implore.
The touch of light can mend the fray,
In Healing Haven, light holds sway.

Beneath the arch of emerald leaves,
A symphony of hope perceives.
The croon, like balm, soothes every wound,
And in its warmth, sweet hearts are tuned.

Where rivers flow with silver gleam,
In twilight's glow, the wonders beam.
The nightingale, with voice so bright,
Calls forth the dawn, dispelling night.

In Healing Haven, time does pause,
With love as deep as ancient laws.
So listen close and do believe,
For in this place, all hearts will cleave.

Nightfall over Scorched Earth

The sun dips low, the shadows creep,
A whisper of the secrets keep.
Nightfall drapes her velvet shroud,
On scars of land that once was proud.

The air hangs thick with tales untold,
Of fire and ash, of courage bold.
The moon, a guardian in the sky,
Watches over, a watchful eye.

Stars start to blink on darkened days,
Illuminating the charred pathways.
In silence, the echoes of pain,
Resound like thunder, fierce as rain.

Yet in the dark, faint glimmers spark,
Of life renewed within the stark.
For every ending breathes a start,
As night enfolds with tender heart.

So heed the night's soft lullaby,
For in its cradle, dreams can fly.
From ashes rise a brighter claim,
In nightfall's grace, rekindle flame.

Grains of Time under a Red Sky

Under the glow of a fiery hue,
The grains of time drift from the blue.
Each moment caught like flecks of dust,
In a tapestry woven with trust.

Winds whisper tales of those gone by,
Their laughter echoing in the sky.
With each heartbeat, stories unfold,
In warmth that ignites the heart of gold.

The red sky bleeds with sunset's sighs,
As day concedes to night's gentle rise.
Time flickers like the flame's soft dance,
Inviting the soul to take a chance.

So gather 'round, let shadows blend,
For every grain, a conscious friend.
Embrace the moments, both near and far,
And guide your dreams like a shooting star.

Under this sky, the world takes flight,
With each grain a memory, pure delight.
Hold fast to time, let love's light beam,
For in each heartbeat, we can dream.

The Awakening of the Phoenix Grove

In dawn's embrace, the grove awakes,
With every leaf, the world remakes.
A spark ignites from ashes gray,
In whispers soft, the phoenix plays.

The branches stretch to greet the morn,
From dreams of night, new life is born.
In colors bright, the flames do gleam,
As nature hums a vibrant dream.

The air is thick with fragrant fire,
That lifts the heart, inspires desire.
In stillness found among the trees,
The phoenix sings upon the breeze.

Here endings do not spell despair,
For life renews with love to share.
With every beat, a cycle spins,
In Phoenix Grove, the story begins.

So walk the path where wonders glide,
With hope and love forever tied.
From ashes rise, let spirits move,
In the awakening, the heart will prove.

Resilience Hidden Beneath the Surface

Beneath the weight of whispered fears,
A strength awakes, defying years.
Roots entwined in darkest soil,
Flowing, thriving, through pain's toil.

In shadows deep, where whispers lie,
Through tempest storms, the brave still try.
Waves may crash, yet tides will shift,
Within the heart, resilience lifts.

Through silence thick, and nights so long,
Emerges truth, unwavering, strong.
With every tear, a spark ignites,
Beneath the waves, a fire alights.

Awake, the spirit, bold and bright,
Defying darkness, claiming light.
For in the depths, a promise blooms,
Resilience thrives amidst the glooms.

So heed the whispers of the deep,
For dreams are sown, while sorrows weep.
With courage, grasp each dawning ray,
Resilience lives, come what may.

Spirits of the Fallen Canopy

In the quiet of the forest's heart,
Where shadows dance and secrets part,
Whispers of leaves, a timeless song,
The spirits dwell, where they belong.

Beneath the boughs, their stories weave,
Of autumn's breath, and winter's eve.
Dancing with dreams, through ages past,
They linger on, in shadows cast.

Through rustling leaves, their laughter calls,
In every hush, a history sprawls.
Guardians of tales, both fierce and sweet,
In fallen canopies, memories meet.

With every gust, they rise and twine,
In the sacred grove, their spirits shine.
Offer a prayer, a nod in the breeze,
And feel their warmth among the trees.

In twilight's glow, their essence stands,
Embraced by earth, entwined with sands.
Listen close, let your heart be free,
For in this realm, their spirits see.

Branches Reaching for Tomorrow

In the embrace of morning light,
Branches stretch with all their might.
Leaves unfurl to greet the day,
In every rustle, hope finds its way.

Roots below, in strength they ground,
While reaching high, where dreams abound.
Though storms may ravage, skies may weep,
Tales of tenacity, the branches keep.

With every gust, they bend and sway,
Yet cling to life in nature's play.
Each knot and curl, a story spun,
Of battles faced and victories won.

In colors bright, they dance and blend,
With whispers soft, and messages to send.
A future waits, just out of sight,
For branches yearning, stretching for light.

Together they rise, a canopy grand,
Fingers intertwined, they take a stand.
With every spring, new dreams in tow,
Branches extend, reaching for tomorrow.

Sparks of Hope from Scattered Remnants

Amidst the ash, where shadows fall,
Sparks of hope begin to call.
From shattered dreams and splintered schemes,
Rise flickers bright, igniting dreams.

In fragments lost, a tale is spun,
Of battles fought, of battles won.
Though scattered wide, the heart can mend,
From every break, new paths extend.

With courage found in every piece,
A light ignites, a soft release.
Gather the remnants, let them shine,
For in their glow, new worlds align.

Through whispered winds and softest cries,
Emerges strength, where silence lies.
For every scar tells stories true,
Of resilience forged, anew, anew.

So cherish the sparks, let embers grow,
In scattered remnants, let hope flow.
With every beat, let hope ascend,
From ashes deep, new beginnings blend.

Whispers of Timber in the Ember Light

In shadows where the old trees sigh,
The whispers of the night draw nigh.
A flicker dances, soft and bright,
Ember light reveals the flight.

Leaves rustle secrets in the dark,
Beneath the stars, an ancient spark.
The wood remembers tales untold,
In every grain, a heart of gold.

From hollow trunks, the silence hums,
As twilight brings its lullaby drums.
The warmth of fire, a gentle glow,
Wraps the forest in a golden show.

Each breeze carries the history's kiss,
In the embrace of the woods, such bliss.
Time sways gently, it seems to bend,
In the light's embrace, all sorrows mend.

So heed the timber's soft refrain,
In amber light, we feel its pain.
Yet in the warmth, we find our place,
Among the spirits of this space.

Echoes of Ash and Ancient Wood

In hollows deep where shadows creep,
Echoes linger, secrets keep.
The ash lies thick, a solemn field,
Where ancient wisdom once was revealed.

The whispers rise with every gust,
Among the roots, in earth we trust.
Old tales woven in bark and bone,
Their echoes guide us, though we roam alone.

Through tangled brambles, the stories wade,
Of battles fought, of voices laid.
The solemn trees, they stand so bold,
Guardians of truths that will never unfold.

Each crack and creak sings of the past,
In whispers soft, the die is cast.
The forest breathes a timeless hymn,
Where heart and history intertwine within.

So walk these paths with open heart,
For every ending is just a part.
Of life's great cycle, tender and true,
As we gather strength from what we pursue.

Charred Leaves Beneath the Soaring Flame

In twilight's hue, the embers glow,
Charred leaves whisper from below.
Beneath the sky where wild dreams soar,
A tale of fire, forevermore.

The flames they dance, a fierce delight,
Consuming shadows, painting night.
Yet from the ashes, life will sprout,
In every spark, there's hope, no doubt.

The glow above, a guiding star,
Reminds us all just who we are.
With every flicker, the fire sings,
Of rebirth, and what tomorrow brings.

In every charred leaf's tender grace,
Lies proof of strength in this vast space.
For through the trials, we rise anew,
Transforming pain, like morning dew.

So fear not the flames that fiercely burn,
For every lesson, we'll surely learn.
Amidst the chaos, the heart will claim,
Its place within the soaring flame.

The Phoenix's Whisper Amidst the Bark

Among the trees, a whisper flows,
Of fiery dreams and ancient prose.
The Phoenix sings from roots so deep,
Awakening those who dare to leap.

In circles spun in ash and dust,
The circle of life, in flame we trust.
With every beat, the heart ignites,
A dance of magic, illuminating nights.

Through branches high, the echoes claim,
The stories woven in the flame.
Each flicker tells a tale so grand,
Of rebirth written in soft sand.

So listen close to what you hear,
The Phoenix calls, it's drawing near.
With every whisper, it invites,
To share our dreams, to climb the heights.

In bark and branch, the flame resides,
Emboldened souls, where hope abides.
For in the forest, magic's spark,
Brings forth the Phoenix, amidst the bark.

Renewal from Grit and Glory

From shadows deep, where spirits dwell,
A spark ignites, a potent spell.
With grit we rise, from ashes torn,
A promise blooms, a new dawn's born.

Through trials faced, with hearts so bold,
We carve our path, let stories unfold.
In strength we trust, amidst the strife,
Emerging whole, we weave our life.

With every step on rugged ground,
The whispers of the past resound.
In victory's light, we shed the night,
Transforming pain into pure delight.

A tapestry of joy and tears,
A symphony that calms our fears.
Together we stand, arms intertwined,
In renewed grace, our strength designed.

So let us dance, let laughter ring,
For from the grit, new glories spring.
With open hearts, we shall embrace,
The beauty found in every space.

Nature's Prayer on the Sooty Ground

Upon the earth, so stained yet bright,
A whisper plays, a soft lamplight.
The soil, rich with ancient lore,
Cradles life, forevermore.

In blooms anew, a hymn resounds,
Through twisted paths, where hope is found.
Each budding sprout a prayer takes flight,
In nature's arms, we seek the light.

The trees stand tall, their branches sway,
In zephyrs soft, they gently lay.
A calling from the depths below,
Where roots entwine in silent glow.

The rain descends, a sacred gift,
To cleanse the earth, our spirits lift.
In droplets clear, the promise wakes,
A dance of life, as stillness breaks.

With every sigh, the wind confides,
A solace found where nature bides.
In harmony, our hearts unite,
To share this prayer, the world alight.

Phoenix Dreams Beneath the Ash

In silent realms, beneath the gray,
Where embers whisper, shadows play.
A phoenix stirs with dreams anew,
From ashen depths, its spirit grew.

With wings outspread, it takes to flight,
A surge of grace, a burst of light.
From every flame, the past it sheds,
In vibrant hues, where courage threads.

The night dissolves, a canvas bright,
Each color sings, ignites the night.
Through fiery storms, it finds its way,
Towards dawn's embrace, a brand new day.

With every beat, a heartbeat strong,
Resilience hums a timeless song.
In whispers soft, ancestral charms,
It dances free, in nature's arms.

So let us dream, beneath the ash,
Transform our fears, let shadows clash.
For in the embers, hope resides,
The phoenix flies, as joy abides.

Ebb and Flow of Fire and Flora

In whispered tales of fire and bloom,
Lives the pulse of life, dispelling gloom.
With every spark, a story sown,
In vibrant fields where dreams have grown.

The dance of flames, a fierce embrace,
Ignites the earth, a warm embrace.
From charred remains, green shoots arise,
In nature's weave, a sweet surprise.

The rhythm sways, like tides of fate,
In gentle cycles, we await.
For every death, a birth shall come,
As whispers fade, new voices hum.

Through seasons shift, the echoes sing,
Of fire and flora, imagining.
A tapestry of scars and grace,
In every heart, a sacred place.

So let us cherish all we find,
The ebb and flow, entwined, aligned.
In every spark, a chance to grow,
With love's embrace, we come to know.

Reclamation of the Verdant Ground

In shadows deep, the seedlings grow,
From ashes cold, a soft green glow.
With whispered winds, they stretch and rise,
To greet the sun in azure skies.

Each stone unturned, a tale unfolds,
Of ancient roots and dreams retold.
The earth, once bare, now sings anew,
A symphony in vibrant hue.

The rivers carve where silence lay,
Through tangled vines, they weave the day.
Nature's hand, both bold and kind,
Reclaims her land, her heart entwined.

And in the glade where light seeps in,
Rebirth begins, a chance to win.
A chorus of life, both fierce and fair,
In every corner, beauty rare.

So plant the seeds of hope and grace,
In every heart, a sacred space.
With tender care, we mend the seams,
Of fractured earth and whispered dreams.

Binding Roots of Destiny

In tangled paths where fate does tread,
The roots of time are gently spread.
They bind our hearts with silent ties,
Connecting souls beneath the skies.

Each choice a thread, both weak and strong,
In woven fates, we all belong.
Yet in the dark, we sometimes stray,
Unraveling dreams that fade away.

But brave the storm, for light shall come,
To guide us back, to beat the drum.
In every twist, in every turn,
A wisdom waits for us to learn.

The stars align, a cosmic dance,
With every moment, a fleeting chance.
So clasp the hands of those you find,
For in their strength, our hearts combined.

Together we grow, unbound, yet whole,
Embracing life, achieving goals.
With roots entwined in love's embrace,
We carve our path, our rightful space.

The Eternal Cycle of Flame and Growth

A spark ignites the silent night,
With warmth that brings both fear and light.
From ember's glow, the ashes lie,
Yet from the soot, new seedlings try.

Fire dances, wild and free,
In chaos lies serenity.
Through trials fierce, the spirit wakes,
In every trial, a path one makes.

Then spring arrives with gentle rain,
To wash away the trials' stain.
The charred remains give way to green,
A cycle graced with life unseen.

From flame we learn, and from the fall,
The heart finds strength to heed the call.
In every cycle, lessons found,
With every flame, a love profound.

And as the seasons shift and weave,
We find the hope we dare believe.
In every dawn, a new chance grows,
To rise anew, as nature knows.

Where the Wildflowers Dare to Bloom

In secret glades where whispers play,
The wildflowers find their way.
With colors bright against the grey,
They paint the world, a bold display.

Amongst the thorns, they take their stand,
With steadfast roots in stubborn land.
They sway and nod, with gentle grace,
Embracing life in every space.

Where sunlight streams and shadows fade,
These humble blooms are unafraid.
They bloom in cracks, in crevices slight,
A testament of hope and light.

And when the storms unleash their tears,
The wildflowers calm our fears.
For in their fragrance, we find peace,
A gentle touch that won't decrease.

So let us learn from nature's art,
To thrive in places set apart.
For where the wildflowers dare to bloom,
Love conquers all, dispelling gloom.

Flickers of Hope Amongst the Remnants

In the ashes where dreams once lay,
New buds awaken, chase gloom away.
Soft whispers of life in desolate nooks,
Nature's embrace, in forgotten books.

Beneath the rubble, a spark ignites,
Determined against the cold, dark nights.
Courage blooms where shadows reside,
Fleeting joys and hopes collide.

Yet still the winds of change might sing,
A melody fresh, on awakening's wing.
Silent promises held in the ground,
Resilience in every heartbeat found.

Through the cracks, the light will seep,
Breaching barriers we wish to keep.
For hope is a seed that defies despair,
With every breath, it calls for care.

So gather up these fragments dear,
The remnants of laughter, a trail of cheer.
In the dance of rebirth, truths unfold,
Amidst the ruins, brave stories told.

Harmony of Flames and Ancient Roots

Where fire meets the ground so cold,
An ancient tale is deftly told.
With flickering warmth and shadows cast,
A union of forces unsurpassed.

Amidst the embers, roots entwine,
Delivering whispers, aged and divine.
The trees sway low, a song of grace,
A fiery dance in nature's embrace.

In the chaos, a rhythm flows,
A pulse of life where the wild wind blows.
Through ash and heat, a strength is grown,
In the heart of the blaze, new seeds are sown.

Each flicker a promise, each spark a sign,
That even in darkness, we shall shine.
For harmony thrives in realms we tread,
Through intertwined stories, both old and spread.

So let the fire dance, let the roots take hold,
In the tale of life, brave and bold.
Together they forge an enduring song,
A tapestry bright where we all belong.

Shadows of Growth Beneath Fiery Wings

In the twilight where shadows play,
Young hearts rise with a bright array.
Fiery wings cast their warm embrace,
As dreams take flight in a timeless race.

Each whispering leaf tells a tale,
Of resilience and strength in the gale.
With every flap, with every sway,
The dance of future lights the way.

Roots burrow deep in the charred ground,
Seeking waters where hope is found.
Beneath the surface, life will weave,
A testament bold to all who believe.

Though shadows linger, the light will rise,
Guiding spirits to the boundless skies.
For within the darkness, beauty again,
Sustained by the warmth of the fiercest flame.

Let us nurture the seeds we've sown,
For beneath the ashes, new dreams are grown.
With fiery wings that shelter our plight,
We flourish anew, embracing the light.

A Testament to Life in Scorched Lands

In lands once vibrant, scorched and bare,
Remnants of life hang in the air.
Yet, tenacious sprouts dare to break,
Defying fate with each step they take.

The sun beats down, relentless flame,
Yet in this harshness, life finds its claim.
With courage engraved in every vein,
The silent whispers of hope remain.

New paths emerge from the crusted earth,
Glimmers of life, a testament of rebirth.
In every crack, in every stone,
A story of struggle, resilience grown.

They rise from the depths, these brave little souls,
Teaching the world of unyielding goals.
For amidst the ruins, there's beauty to find,
In the dance of survival, love intertwined.

So let us honor those fierce hearts alive,
In the scorched lands where dreams strive.
For life endures, against all odds,
A testament etched in the hands of gods.

Charred Memories Beneath the Stars

In the hush of night, we stand so still,
Whispers of the past, a haunting thrill.
Beneath the stars, our secrets lay bare,
Charred memories linger, heavy in the air.

Echoes of laughter, once bright as day,
Now dance in shadows, drifting away.
The echoes flicker like embers aglow,
Under the vast sky, where lost moments flow.

Each flicker of light tells a tale untold,
Of dreams intertwined, both timid and bold.
As we weave our stories through the cool night,
Charred memories shimmer, caught in their flight.

Time molds our hearts as seasons unfold,
Turning our warmth into tales of old.
Yet in every scar, there's a lesson learned,
Under the stars, the fire still burned.

So let us remember, amidst the vast sky,
The warmth of our stories that never say die.
For beneath the starlight, we'll always unite,
In the charred memories that spark our delight.

The Sizzle of Old Flames

The crackle of fire, a sound so sweet,
Whispers of love in the heat we meet.
Old flames flicker, with warmth from the past,
In the sizzle and smoke, our shadows are cast.

Twilight descends, painting skies deep blue,
Every spark carries the essence of you.
In the dance of the flames, stories reignite,
With every soft glow, the memories take flight.

Through the glowing embers, I see your face,
In the flickering light, I find my place.
Moments entwined in a fiery embrace,
The sizzle of old flames, our hearts interlaced.

Yet with the dawn, the embers turn cold,
The warmth of our love, still bravely bold.
But deep in my heart, where the fire still glows,
The sizzle of old flames forever shows.

So gather around, let the stories flow,
Of old flames and whispers, let the memories grow.
For in every flicker lies a cherished refrain,
The sizzle of old flames will always remain.

Scars of the Resilient Earth

In the heart of the land, scars tell a tale,
Of storms that have raged and winds that prevail.
The earth bears witness to trials endured,
With resilience blooming, forever assured.

Mountains stand tall, though weathered and worn,
Majestic reminders of battles they've borne.
Through valleys of shadows, life finds a way,
Scars of the resilient earth light up the day.

Rivers run deep, carving paths anew,
Their waters, a symbol of strength in the blue.
Each ripple, a story, each wave, a song,
The scars of the earth remind us we're strong.

Beneath the grey skies, seeds push through stone,
Sprouting hope where the winds have blown.
For every lost moment, a future unfolds,
Scars of the land, their beauty retold.

So let us listen to the whispers of ground,
In cracks and in crevices, resilience found.
For the earth is our home, forever we'll tread,
Honoring scars where the stories have led.

Cinders Amidst the Evergreen

Among the green trees, cinders lay still,
Silent reminders of passion and will.
Lost in the forest where wildflowers grow,
Cinders of fires, memories aglow.

Whispers of smoke weave through branches high,
As shadows of memories dance in the sky.
Each flicker of light in the twilight gleams,
Cinders amidst the evergreen hold our dreams.

They speak of the warmth that once kissed the air,
Of laughter and joy, a time we can share.
But nature's embrace, with a gentle caress,
Is healing our hearts, bringing solace, no less.

Through seasons they weather, indifferent to time,
Cinders and trees blend in rhythm and rhyme.
In the quiet of night, under stars' gentle gleam,
The cinders remind us that hope's never deemed.

So stand with me here, where the old stories burn,
In cinders and greens, we shall slowly learn.
That life's fleeting embers may fade away fast,
But love's gentle spark will forever hold fast.

Shadows on the Ground of Renewal

In twilight's soft embrace they creep,
Whispers of the night so deep.
With every step, the secrets stir,
Beneath the stars, the shadows were.

A dance of light, a flicker bright,
Awakens dreams in quiet night.
Among the roots, the magic breathes,
In silent songs, the spirit weaves.

Through veils of dusk, a promise gleams,
Of life renewed in silver streams.
Each shadow cast, a tale untold,
A future bright, a heart of gold.

Underneath the moon's soft gaze,
The earth begins its healing phase.
With every pulse, with every sound,
The hopes of spring rise from the ground.

So let these shadows guide the way,
Through darkened woods where lost dreams lay.
For in each step, the past must yield,
To open hearts and fertile fields.

When the Forest Met the Fire

In embers' glow, where shadows dance,
The forest stood, caught in the trance.
Crimson flames, a fierce, wild song,
Nature's heart beats fierce and strong.

Whispers raged through branches high,
As ashes fell from a smoky sky.
Yet every burn holds untold grace,
Refresh the earth, a warm embrace.

From charred remains, new life will sprout,
In every seed, a silent shout.
The fire's wrath, a cruel hand,
But in its wake, healing will stand.

So nature weeps, yet learns to rise,
Beneath the gray, new life complies.
For every end, a new design,
A cycle spun through space and time.

When fire claims what once was green,
A truth is found, though seldom seen.
In ashes lie the dreams reborn,
Of brighter days, and hope's new dawn.

Forgotten Echoes of the Past

In shadows deep where silence dwells,
Time's whispered tales like distant bells.
Through crumbling walls, the stories flow,
Of hearts once bold, now dust and low.

Echoes fade in twilight's hush,
The past lingers in a quiet rush.
Lost loves and battles, dreams once grand,
Held in the palm of an ancient hand.

Ghostly figures dance in light,
Fleeting visions, just out of sight.
Each breath a memory, soft and frail,
The heart beats on, an endless trail.

In every glance, a yearning spark,
To find the flame within the dark.
For what was lost can still remain,
In echoes sweet, in joy and pain.

So let us tread with gentle care,
The paths where shadows ever stare.
For in the silence, we shall hear,
The voices faint, yet ever near.

The Resurgence of Nature's Heart

In meadows green where flowers bloom,
The earth awakens from its gloom.
Soft breezes hum a joyful tune,
As life returns beneath the moon.

With each new dawn, the sunlight pours,
A golden brush on open doors.
The rivers rush, the skies grow clear,
In every heart, a song to cheer.

The trees stand tall, their branches sway,
Reclaiming hope in bright array.
With whispers sweet, the wind will play,
As nature's heart beats night and day.

Through fields of dreams, the spirits roam,
In every petal, life finds home.
A tapestry of colors bright,
Awakens every soul in flight.

So come and walk where magic lives,
In every breath, the heart still gives.
For nature's pulse will never cease,
In every moment, find your peace.

The Spirit of Wood Beneath Burning Skies

In twilight's glow, the shadows creep,
The spirit of wood sings soft and deep.
With burning skies that blush and fade,
Whispers of magic in the glade.

Beneath the boughs where secrets dwell,
Old tales are spun, the air a spell.
The ember's dance in evening's chill,
Calls forth the dreams, the heart's own will.

Leaves flutter down, like wishes untold,
Each carrying stories of brave and bold.
The forest hums a tune revered,
While stars awaken, lightly peered.

As twilight thickens, wraps the night,
The spirit glows with ethereal light.
In quiet corners, deep and wide,
The ancient woods, our joy and pride.

So let the fire crackle and sigh,
For beneath these skies, the wood shall lie.
In every ember, warmth remains,
A timeless bond through joys and pains.

Phantoms of the Past in Glimmering Ash

In the hush of night, the past awakes,
Phantoms of love in shimmering lakes.
They dance on the breeze, in whispers soft,
Memories linger, aloft, aloft.

Ashen remains of stories spun,
Glimmering fragments of battles won.
The flicker of fire, the crackle of fate,
Brings echoes of laughter that won't abate.

Through shadowy corners, they twirl and glide,
On the strings of time, where dreams reside.
In every curl of smoke that plays,
Lives a legacy of yesterdays.

Yet here in the glow, we find our way,
In glimmering ash, we choose to stay.
With hands held tight, we face the dawn,
And with each breath, the phantoms yawn.

So let us gather 'round the flame,
In tales of old, we find our name.
For in their glow, our hearts shall bask,
In light and love, no need to ask.

Cerulean Dreams Amidst Charred Timbers

In a world of dreams, cerulean hues,
Amidst charred timbers, hope renews.
Beneath the ash, a spark does glow,
Timeless stories of long ago.

With eyes alight like stars above,
We wander through the realms of love.
Amongst the echoes, angels play,
In charred remains, they find their way.

Through twilight's veil, where shadows blend,
In cerulean hues, we claim our end.
Old wounds may heal in night's embrace,
While dreams unite in a warm trace.

So let the embers crackle bright,
As dreams awaken in the night.
In whispered tones, the past is near,
What once was lost, now draws us here.

Together, through the smoke we soar,
In cerulean dreams forevermore.
Amidst charred timbers, life resumes,
In every heart, new love blooms.

Tales of the Hearth's Embrace

In the hearth's embrace, tales of old,
Stories of warmth and courage bold.
With every crackle, a new dream spins,
In flickering flames, the night begins.

The stories weave like threads of gold,
In whispered echoes, their truths unfold.
Laughter dances in the flicker light,
Binding us close, through the dark of night.

With shadows playing on the wall,
We gather round, the warmth our call.
Each tale a treasure, a gem to keep,
In the hearth's embrace, we softly weep.

For love is the fire, fierce and bright,
It warms the heart through the coldest night.
In every flicker, hope ignites,
In the hearth's embrace, love alights.

So let the stories swirl and twine,
In the dance of flames, our souls align.
With tales of the hearth, forever shared,
In every ember, a heart prepared.

Old Trunks with New Stories

In the forest deep where secrets lie,
Old trunks whisper tales as the winds sigh.
Bark worn and weathered, a life well told,
In rings of time, their memories unfold.

Moss-clad and stoic, they stand as friends,
Guardians of moments, where time rarely bends.
Each creak and groan, a soft-spoken lore,
Of lovers and dreamers who wandered before.

Beneath tangled roots, stories intertwine,
Of joy and of sorrow, like vintage fine wine.
The sun dances freely through leaves overhead,
Casting shadows of dreams on the ground where they tread.

In twilight's embrace, the lights flicker bright,
As fireflies waltz, bringing magic to night.
The old trunks remember, and with them we share,
A tapestry woven with stories laid bare.

So pause for a moment, let silence align,
With echoes of laughter that once were divine.
For old trunks with new stories forever persist,
In the heart of the forest, where shadows exist.

A Tapestry of Fire and Life

Around the hearth, where stories ignite,
Flames dance and twirl, casting shadows of light.
Each flicker reveals, with its vibrant embrace,
A tapestry woven of life's gentle grace.

Embers are whispering tales from the past,
Of laughter and love that was meant to last.
The crackle of wood sings a melodious song,
For every bright flame, memories belong.

As smoke rises softly, it carries a thread,
Of hopes and of dreams that are lovingly spread.
In the heart of the fire, a warmth intertwines,
Binding all that once was in radiant lines.

In flickering moments, we find our true selves,
With stories of heroes and magical elves.
The fire envelops us in warmth and delight,
A tapestry of life woven softly each night.

So sit by the flames, let your spirit take flight,
For in every spark, there's a story in sight.
A tapestry woven with love, joy, and strife,
Embracing our journeys, our fire, our life.

Bright Beginnings in Ashen Places

In places where shadows and ashes reside,
New beginnings flicker, like stars that collide.
The earth may be barren, yet hope takes its flight,
From seeds long forgotten, towards luminous light.

With whispers of winds through the desolate trees,
In stillness and silence, we find hidden pleas.
Life breathes in softly, rejuvenates the land,
Brick by brick, it rises, by nature's own hand.

Amongst the charred remains, bright colors emerge,
Life dances anew, like an unstoppable surge.
Petals of courage, in colors so bold,
Painting the landscape that once was left cold.

In ash-laden corners, we nurture our dreams,
With love as our anchor, life bursts at the seams.
From cinders, we gather the strength to begin,
To build on the dreams, where the past had been thin.

So cherish each moment, let spirits rejoice,
For in ashen places, we find our true voice.
Bright beginnings rise from the remnants of pain,
With faith as our compass, we flourish again.

The Secret Life of Charred Logs

In the heart of the forest, beneath shadows laced,
Charred logs lie quiet, with secrets embraced.
Beneath their rough edges, stories are spun,
Of battles and friendships, of lost and of won.

Underneath the surface, a world full of grace,
Life finds a way in this unyielding space.
Moss blankets the wood, while time patiently weaves,
A tapestry vibrant, where laughter believe.

The charred and the blackened hold warmth of the sun,
In cracks of their bark, an adventure begun.
For nature is patient, and life will return,
From ashes, a flame, where passion will burn.

Each log is a chapter, a page turned with care,
A testament living, where few would dare stare.
In silence they whisper, of journeys they've shared,
The life of the forest, always unpaired.

So honor the logs, with their stories untold,
For in their still presence, there's magic to hold.
The secret life thrives in the depths of the wood,
In charred hearts and souls, life speaks if it could.

Whispers of the Embered Grounds

Beneath the moon's soft glow, they sigh,
The voices of ages, passing by.
In shadows deep, the secrets lark,
A tapestry woven, a flickering spark.

With every crackle, a tale unfolds,
Of heroes, lost and legends bold.
In embers bright, the past ignites,
Whispers murmuring in the night.

Through the bramble and thicket, they creep,
Of dreams long buried, and promises to keep.
The ground, a keeper of echoes dear,
In every crack, a memory near.

As the dawn approaches with gentle grace,
The embers fade, but not their trace.
For in the heart, the whispers stay,
Guiding the weary upon their way.

So heed the call of the embered ground,
In every whisper, a truth is found.
With every step on this ancient path,
Embrace the stories, feel their wrath.

Ashen Trails of Time

On ashen trails where shadows dwell,
The lingering echoes weave a spell.
With every footfall, stories sigh,
Of yesteryears that never die.

Cloaked in mist, the journey unfolds,
In hushed tones, the past softly scolds.
Guiding the wanderers, light and dark,
Each step holds a promise, a hidden spark.

Through tangled woods where secrets lay,
Every leaf holds the hues of grey.
The whispers of time brush past like smoke,
In the heart of the silence, a story bespoke.

A fleeting glimpse of what once was here,
In the dance of the shadows, we draw near.
Embers of wisdom etched in the dust,
Along ashen trails, in time we trust.

So walk with care on these weathered ways,
As the history breathes, it quietly sways.
In every moment, the past will gleam,
On ashen trails, we chase the dream.

Echoes from the Wooded Remnants

In the heart of groves where silence reigns,
Echoes wander through soft, verdant chains.
Among the branches, whispers swirl,
Of forgotten tales in a misty whirl.

Each rustling leaf a story weaves,
Of sunlit glades and autumn eves.
In shaded nooks where secrets bloom,
A symphony plays, dispelling gloom.

The roots embrace the tales of yore,
In every creak, a plea for more.
Of creatures small and giants tall,
Their presence felt in the stillness all.

As twilight falls, the echoes breathe,
The woods alive with the tales beneath.
In hushed reveries of night's embrace,
Dreams take flight in this sacred space.

So linger awhile in the wooded shade,
Where echoes of legends serenely fade.
In every shadow, the past we find,
In whispers hidden, forever entwined.

Flakes of History in the Breeze

In the gentle breeze, the past will sway,
Flakes of history drift and play.
Each whisper a promise, each sigh a song,
A dance of moments where we belong.

Like snowflakes swirling in twilight's glow,
The tales of time in the currents flow.
Embroidered in whispers, memories weave,
In the stories shared, we learn to believe.

With every gust, a fragment flies,
Carried softly beneath the skies.
For in the air, the past alights,
A tapestry spun of days and nights.

As voices murmur through the trees,
The gentle echoes ride the breeze.
In fleeting moments, we grasp and see,
The dance of history, wild and free.

So pause and listen, let the flakes glide,
For in their journey, the past won't hide.
In every breath, their stories frame,
Flakes of history whisper your name.

Sublime Reflections in the Ashes

In the quiet grove where shadows loom,
The echoes linger, our dreams consume.
Beneath the stars, our whispers fall,
Like fading embers, answering the call.

The winds carry tales of what once was,
In this hallowed ground, we pause because.
Time unveils the secrets of the past,
In glowing reverie, memories cast.

Ghostly figures dance in the night,
A tapestry woven with pale moonlight.
They spin their stories, how they've endured,
In the ashes of time, the heart is assured.

Reflections shimmer, a mirror's grace,
Lost in the remnants, we find our place.
Through the fleeting moments, we take a stand,
In the face of shadows, united we'll band.

So let the night cradle all our fears,
In the sublime, we'll dry our tears.
As dawn approaches, the past we hold,
Will melt into light, a dream retold.

Forgotten Seasons of the Enchanted Yard

In the garden where whispers of spring once bloomed,
Petals fell softly, like secrets entombed.
The air carries echoes of laughter and light,
In the charm of the seasons, all felt so right.

Summer's embrace held the shimmer of days,
Among the tall grasses, lost in their ways.
Fireflies danced as twilight unfurled,
In forgotten seasons, we cherished our world.

Autumn then painted with hues of gold,
Leaves like confetti in stories retold.
Memory weaves through the branches that sway,
Bearing witness to dreams that won't fade away.

Winter brought silence, a blanket of white,
Stars glittered softly in the depth of the night.
Yet beneath the frost, life still remained,
In roots of the past, love was sustained.

So visit this yard where time softly rests,
In its quiet corners, the heart is blessed.
For in every season, there lies a chance,
To find joy in memories, in a gentle dance.

Roots Beneath the Scorched Surface

Where the earth has cracked and the shadows creep,
Beneath the scorched surface, old secrets sleep.
Roots intertwine in a dance of despair,
Holding the whispers that haunt the air.

In the silence, stories of struggle remain,
Of what had flourished, now lost in the pain.
Yet resilience thrives in the depths of the land,
A promise of life in the touch of a hand.

Searing the soil, the sun's cruel gaze,
Yet nature's magic finds curious ways.
Amidst barren heartaches, hope's spirit stirs,
Awakening green where the heart still purrs.

Though ashes may blanket the fields of our past,
In shadows of sorrow, we still find a cast.
For deep in the soil, the strength will revive,
And from scorched remains, we shall learn to thrive.

So let us remember the roots we can't see,
For within those chambers runs life's decree.
A haven of wonders, both patient and wise,
In the sanctuary hidden 'neath sunburnt skies.

Flickering Dreams Amidst the Embers

In the heart of the night, where shadows dance,
Flickering dreams chance a daring romance.
Embers like starlit wishes alight,
Guiding the lost through the cloak of the night.

Each spark tells a story, of wishes once made,
Of laughter and love that will never fade.
Amidst the ashes, a flicker of hope,
Daring the weary to dream and to cope.

Whispers of magic drift through the air,
Inviting the dreamers to rise and to dare.
For every small spark holds a tale yet unsung,
In the symphony silent, their voices are strung.

With hearts wide open, we chase down the glow,
Following dreams where the wild lilies grow.
In the flickering fires, our spirits unite,
Breathing life into darkness, igniting the night.

So gather the courage, embrace the unknown,
For flickering dreams flourish when shared and grown.
Amidst all the embers, let passions ignite,
In the tapestry woven, there lies purest light.

Worn Paths in the Glow of Renewal

Beneath the trees, where whispers dwell,
Old stones recall a tale to tell.
Roots entwined in secrets old,
While new dreams bloom, their hopes unfold.

The path winds softly, mossy and deep,
Where shadows linger, and memories seep.
Each footstep echoes in gentle refrain,
A journey taken, in joy and pain.

Blades of grass, kissed by the dew,
Glisten in light, fresh and new.
Time weaves threads of silver and gold,
In this sacred space, our stories unfold.

The sun dips low, a fiery hue,
Embracing the world with a soft adieu.
As night descends, stars ignite the night,
Guiding our hearts with their twinkling light.

So walk with me where spirits rise,
In the glow of renewal beneath the skies.
With every step, let us reclaim,
The worn paths, forever the same.

Markings of Time on Weathered Grain

Carved and etched by nature's hand,
Each line a story, a shifting sand.
Grains of wisdom, time's tender trace,
In wooden whispers, we find our place.

Seasons pass, their breath entwined,
In every knot, a truth defined.
The dance of ages, a silent song,
In the heart of wood, where we belong.

Beneath the bark, secrets hide,
In every ring, the years collide.
Witness to laughter, to sorrow's pain,
The markings of time on weathered grain.

A gentle breeze, the leaves respond,
To echoes of those who have long gone.
In nature's tale, we carve our dreams,
While sunlight softens the moonlit beams.

So let us gather, in this embrace,
With stories spun in nature's grace.
For each grain tells of love and loss,
In the markings of time, we find our cause.

Flickering Shadows in the Forest's Heart

In tangled woods where silence sings,
Flickering shadows dance on wings.
The hush of night wraps around tight,
As creatures stir beneath the light.

Moonbeams weave through branches high,
Painting dreams against the sky.
In whispered tones, the forest speaks,
Of ancient truths and hidden streaks.

The rustle of leaves, a gentle sigh,
As night unfolds, and stars draw nigh.
Beneath the canopy, a world unseen,
Where magic dwells, and spirits gleam.

A fox darts past in a flash of red,
Seeking solace where the wild things tread.
Each flicker reveals a tale to tell,
In the heart of the forest, where shadows dwell.

So linger here, where mysteries reign,
In the flickering shadows, let joy remain.
For in the dark, a spark ignites,
A bond with wonder, under starry nights.

A Dance of Briars Beneath the Sky

In tangled thorns, a dance does start,
Beneath the sky, a wild heart.
The briars twine, a woven maze,
In nature's grip, we find our ways.

With every step, the brambles sing,
Of hopes entwined and love's sweet sting.
Petals blush 'neath the thorny lace,
As beauty hides in a fierce embrace.

The stars above, they watch in grace,
As shadows twirl in a gentle space.
The night unfolds with secrets rare,
In this dance of briars, hearts laid bare.

Through tangled paths, let courage roam,
For even the briars find a home.
In every cut, a story gains,
Of resilience grown in love's sweet strains.

So dance with me, as twilight sighs,
In the embrace of the starlit skies.
For in the briars, beauty we find,
A tapestry woven, hearts intertwined.

Where Echoes and Embers Entwine

In the forest deep, where shadows play,
Whispers of old, drift soft and gray.
Memories linger like dew on leaves,
Carried by winds, in twilight it weaves.

Beneath the stars, where silence sings,
The tales of the night spread their wings.
Flickers of fire, beneath the moon's gaze,
Stirring the heart in a flickering blaze.

Among rugged stones, where the owls call,
Echoes of laughter, now faint, now small.
A path of embers beneath weary feet,
Lies softly waiting for souls to meet.

Hushed whispers blend with ancient bark,
Tales of forgotten, long lost in the dark.
Where echoes meet embers, a dance so divine,
In shadows of trees, our spirits entwine.

So linger awhile, let the moonlight guide,
Through forests of memory, where dreams abide.
For in the night's hush, we find our place,
In the embrace of the ember's grace.

Overshadowed but Not Overcome

In the winding paths of tangled fate,
Shadows may linger, but hope won't wait.
In the darkest corners of our mind,
Light peeks through, its warmth defined.

Though storms may rage and winds may howl,
Strength is found in the silent growl.
With every setback, a step we take,
More resilient hearts begin to wake.

Over mountains high and valleys low,
The seed of courage begins to grow.
With layers thick, fears come undone,
Battles are fought until victory's won.

In the shadows cast by fearsome night,
We rise like suns, prepared to fight.
Every stumble and every fall,
Leads us to wisdom, answers call.

From ashes we rise, a phoenix unchained,
In trials of fire, our spirits are trained.
Though overshadowed, we shine ever bright,
Reflecting the truth, embracing the light.

The Colorful Echo of Flame

Colors dance in the ember's glow,
A spectrum rich, where passions flow.
Orange and red in a fervent embrace,
Whirling and twirling in radiant space.

With every crackle, a story unfolds,
Of brave hearts and dreams, and legends bold.
The whispers of flame, a vibrant tune,
Residing beneath the watchful moon.

In flickers and sparks, our wishes take flight,
Igniting the soul in the depth of the night.
Each hue tells a tale, a vibrant refrain,
Echoing softly in the heart of the flame.

Through the night skies where shadows retreat,
The embers create a place so sweet.
For in the dance of their fiery bliss,
Lie the colorful echoes we find in a kiss.

So gather around, let the stories unfold,
In each glowing ember, the warmth becomes gold.
For where colors arise, our hopes do reclaim,
The colorful echo of life's flickering flame.

New Beginnings from Sear and Smolder

In the ashes of yesterdays quietly lay,
Whispers of promise in shades of gray.
From the embers' glow, new visions ignite,
Hopes that were hidden now take to flight.

Each scar tells a tale, a journey begun,
Paths paved with courage, battles hard-won.
In the heart of despair, a spark is born,
From sear and smolder, the new day is sworn.

With every dawn, we rise from the haze,
Chasing the light through the twilight's maze.
In the ashes' warmth, possibility calls,
As roots push deeper, and the spirit enthralls.

New chapters await, the ink freshly spilled,
With dreams to explore and futures fulfilled.
For the fire inside is a beacon so bright,
Guiding our hearts through the long, starry night.

So gather your courage, let go of the past,
For new beginnings await, free and vast.
In the dance of rebirth, we shall find our way,
From sear and smolder, a glorious day.